NEW NORWAY

On the verge of a new millennium

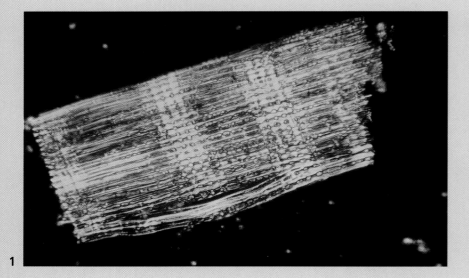

1

2

3

Population (1.1.96):	4.4 million

Largest cities:

Oslo	488 659
Bergen	223 238
Trondheim	143 829
Stavanger	104 373

Life expectancy:

Women	80.6 years
Men	74.8 years

Surface area:

Mainland Norway	386 975 sq.km
Continental shelf	1 194 810 sq.km
Svalbard	62 700 sq.km

Distribution of area (per cent):

Mountains	62
Productive forest	22
Agricultural land	3
Islands, lakes, glaciers, cities	13

Midnight Sun:

Harstad	25 May-17 July
North Cape	12 May-29 July

Employment by industry (per cent)

Agriculture	4.2
Fishing	0.9
Industry/oil	15.9
Construction	6.1
Services	70.2
Other	2.7

Gross domestic product 1995:   NOK 923 billion
(USD 146 billion)

Some key Norwegian products reveal an unusual and surprising array of colours under the microscope. These pictures have been taken in polarised light, magnified 40 times.

1 The structure of Norway's most important commercial tree species, the spruce. Trees must carry water and nutrients through their trunks and branches. Both vertical and transverse transport channels can be seen.

2 Cellulose fibres magnified 100 times. Products based on forest raw materials have played an important role in Norwegian industrial development.

GDP per head: NOK 211 890 (USD 33 446)

Foreign trade (in NOK billion):

Exports	353
Crude oil and natural gas	112
Metals	29
Mechanical engineering	29
Fish	19
Shipping	45
Other services	42
Imports	297
Trade balance on current account	32

Most important market areas (per cent)

European Union	75
Rest of Europe	5
Other industrial countries	11
Developing countries	9

Merchant fleet 1.1.96:
Norway has the world's sixth largest merchant fleet, with 4.5 per cent of total tonnage.

1 385 ships totalling 47 mill dwt

Under Norwegian flag	960 ships
Under other flags	425 ships

91 ships of 5.1 mill dwt under construction or on order

At Norwegian yards	19 ships

Petroleum production 1995: 162 million tonnes of oil equivalents (toe)
Oil exports: 132 million toe/2.7 million barrels per day

Norway is the world's second largest oil exporter after Saudi Arabia.

3 Crystallised vanillin. Originally a by-product of chemical pulp production at Borregaard in Sarpsborg south of Oslo, this is now an important export commodity. Borregaard meets 16-17 per cent of world demand.

4 Zinc bacitracin. Small quantities boost animal appetite and growth. Alpharma has developed this substance as a feed additive.

5 Surface of a pyrite crystal. More than 200 000 tonnes of this mineral are produced annually in Norway.

6 Urea is used both for artificial fertiliser and in industrial applications. Norsk Hydro is one of the world's leading suppliers.

4

5

6

A millennium of money (end papers). Norway's oldest coins are reproduced on the far left. King Olav Tryggvason minted the first, probably in autumn 995. Today's coins, dated a thousand years later, are on the far right. Norway's coinage has been minted by the Royal Mint at Kongsberg west of Oslo since 1686.

Early exports (right). Products from the far north were in demand from the earliest times, and no gift was more popular with European royalty than gyrfalcons. Falconry was the sport of kings. These birds are a protected species today, and attempts to smuggle them out of Norway are severely punished. This female gyrfalcon was photographed in Dividal national park in northern Norway's Troms county.

Telemark-style (title page). Norwegians may not be born with skis on their feet, or on the deck of a boat, but they come into this world at no great distance from ski tracks or pleasure craft. Modern skiing originated in the south-eastern county of Telemark. The special skiing style associated with this region has spread like wildfire through the world's Alpine skiing centres in recent years, and is now a competitive discipline in its own right.

NEW NORWAY 9

On the verge of a new millennium

By Gunnar Jerman

Translated by Rolf Gooderham

NORWEGIAN TRADE COUNCIL

CONTENTS

Fine catch. Salmon fishing in Norwegian rivers made the country famous among the world's
leading anglers, and most foreigners still associate angling in Norway with salmon. However, sea fishing from boat
or shore is growing in popularity. Often yielding far larger catches, it can be pursued year-round.
This spring cod caught off Senja in northern Norway weighed in at 25 kilograms – which
helps to explain why sea angling has become so fashionable.

FROM POVERTY TO PROSPERITY

The North Way – Norvegr – was the name given to this mountainous country by the first seafarers to sail along its rugged shores, which stretched away to the northernmost limits of the world. Adventurers from the south found great wealth there: animals with valuable fur, walruses sporting sought-after tusks and big schools of whales. The early Norwegians exploited these resources and took them along on their voyages into the wide world. Close to a millennium ago, northern Norway also became one of the main suppliers of fish to the growing urban population of continental Europe. The country has since remained one of the world's leading fishing nations.

All countries are different, but some are more different than others. Viewed at a distance, Norway lies so far off the beaten track that it has problems getting on the world map. Only four million inhabitants occupy a country which looks out to the Arctic Ocean, and which should actually be covered with snow and ice. Nowhere else do people live permanently so far to the north. But the climate along the coast is not particularly cold, thanks to the Gulf Stream. This great current carries masses of warmer water along the Norwegian coast to keep it ice-free all year round.

Many foreigners on their first visit to Norway find the country is not what they expected, whether they reach Oslo by car from Sweden, by ship from Germany, Britain or Denmark, or by air. They see few signs of the fjords and mountains celebrated in the tourist brochures, but quickly observe the prosperity of both city and countryside – carefully-tended residential districts, modern commercial buildings and shopping centres, and well-run farms.

Only when they travel west or north do they encounter the scenic splendours made familiar by tourist literature and postcards. It would be hard to find such captivating landscapes and such marked contrasts anywhere else. With a small population spread over one of Europe's large land areas, Norway can offer a closeness to nature and opportunities for outdoor activities that few others can match.

The last half of our present century has witnessed the longest and strongest period of growth ever for Norway's economy and Norwegian industry. These years probably rank as the richest in the country's history, and perhaps also the

Frozen energy. Hydropower has been called "white coal". Since the beginning of this century, the energy of falling water has provided the basis for some of Norway's most important export industries. The bold winter climber on the left is using the 220-metre-high Muldal waterfall in the west coast region of Sunnmøre for something rather more hazardous than energy generation.

Mammoth move. The Troll A gas platform ranks as the tallest structure ever moved. Standing 472 metres from its base to the top of the drilling derrick, this structure is seen here under tow to its destination in the North Sea west of Bergen. There it will stand for many decades to produce one of the world's largest offshore gas fields.

best – whether measured by gross domestic product and other economic indicators, or by human values.

Many people admittedly hark back to the "good old days", but we might reasonably ask: good for whom? It is easy to forget that Norway was a poor country 50 years ago, and had little other than toil and deprivation to offer a significant proportion of its population.

We have no more idea than our ancestors a thousand years ago where the new millennium that faces us will lead. People have never enjoyed greater opportunities than today, yet destroying the accumulated achievements of the past has never been easier.

Today's world is experiencing more upheaval and change than many want to see. Norway has not escaped such problems. The truth is that even an affluent society lacks the resources to fulfil every need. All the same, the country's economic prospects look bright. The economy is booming, Norwegian products are in demand and command good prices, inflation is insignificant, unemployment is declining and offshore revenues allow the government to run a substantial budget surplus. Few dark clouds loom on the horizon at the moment, although recession in Norway's principal European markets could naturally have an impact.

Throughout Norwegian history, the country has depended on economic links with other nations. Even the Viking monarchs whose doings are chronicled in the ancient Saga histories needed revenues from abroad to develop the country, and the state of the wider European economy soon affected living standards in Norway. The Norwegian kings forged trade links with other nations in the early Middle Ages, and Norway's first commercial treaty – with England – was signed as early as 1217. So the country's close economic ties with the rest of Europe date much further back than today's market links and internationalisation.

In a referendum held during November 1994, 52.4 per cent of Norwegian voters rejected membership of the European Union for the second time in 22 years. Conflicting interests between central and peripheral regions of the country were very important for this outcome. While the EU received strong support in the densely populated area around the Oslo Fjord, the anti-membership vote exceeded 70 per cent in each of the three northern counties.

Despite the decision to stay outside the EU, Norwegians feel a community of interest with Europe and want to play a part in developing this region. Collaboration is regulated by the European Economic Area agreement between the EU and Norway as a member of the former European Free Trade Association (Efta). This deal solves most of the problems posed for Norwegian industry by non-membership of the Union. But some important export sectors – notably fishing – continue to be hit by EU regulations.

Dust-free. A number of advanced companies have emerged from the technical community around the former Kongsberg Våpenfabrikk company west of Oslo. Clean-room procedures are essential at Kongsberg Gruppen, which produces the Penguin missile system for warships, fighters and helicopters.

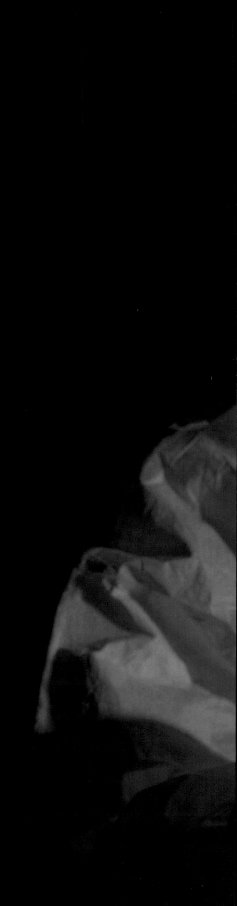

Magic morning. Many foreigners get their first sight of Norway from the passenger ships that sail regularly to and from Denmark, Germany or Britain. Approaching Oslo by sea during the summer ranks as one of the great tourist experiences, but a scene like this is much rarer. Color Line ferry Prinsesse Ragnhild sails up the Oslo Fjord on a Christmas morning, with the winter sun setting the frost smoke afire.

Norway's gross domestic product rose from NOK 10 billion in 1946 to NOK 774 billion in 1994, a sixfold increase when the change in money value is discounted. During this period, a substantial proportion of the labour force moved from primary industries to the manufacturing and service sectors.

Farmers accounted for 20 per cent of the gainfully employed population in 1945, but are now down to four per cent. Fishing employs only 0.9 per cent of the labour force. But fish exports have never been worth more. Services account for 70 per cent of today's jobs, although the number of seafarers has declined substantially. Such structural changes have naturally meant upheavals for large groups of Norwegians, but the country's settlement pattern has remained far more dispersed than the figures might suggest.

Several important events have had a crucial impact on the structure of Norwegian industry over the past 25 years. Huge technological strides, particularly in computing and communications, have made their mark on society. But developments in two new industries – offshore oil and fish farming – can be said to divide the past 50 years into separate eras.

In 1992, three representatives from US oil company Phillips Petroleum visited Trygve Lie, then Norway's industry minister but better known abroad as the first UN secretary-general. The Americans wanted sole rights to all oil exploration in Norway, but were turned down. This application gave further impetus to the job of delineating the boundary for economic operations in the waters off Norway and to work on framing a Norwegian Petroleum Act.

Several years later, a group of foreign oil companies – including Phillips – won licences to explore for oil. Norway ranks today as a substantial oil and gas producer, with three million barrels of oil flowing from its continental shelf every day in 1996. The country is second only to Saudi Arabia as an oil exporter.

Dwarfed in a majestic landscape. Mountain hiking is a popular leisure activity both summer and winter in Norway. The Norwegian highlands present visitors with powerful images and grand experiences. Humans must adapt to nature in such a landscape, because its forces can be violent when unleashed. A group of skiers (above) makes its way into the Rondane range in east central Norway.

Norway's other major advance has been in fish farming, or aquaculture. This business took off about the same time that oil made its entry in the Norwegian economy, but was naturally overshadowed by the offshore industry. But few countries are so well-placed to go on developing the farmed fish business. Trials with new species have been encouraging, although experience from salmon shows that it takes long-term effort and patience to domesticate wild fish.

The significance of aquaculture today – and undoubtedly in the future – should not be underestimated. Over the past 25 years, this industry has become a cornerstone of the coastal economy and is set to become just as important to these communities as traditional fishing. Some optimists believe aquaculture could come to employ as many people as farming and offshore production.

Economic growth over the past century has made Norway a wealthy nation. Many industrial countries are burdened by substantial budget deficits and have

problems maintaining costly welfare systems. By contrast, the main question in Norway's economic debate is how the government's budget surplus should be applied. If politicians succeed in resisting pressures to spend these revenues as soon as they are earned, they can be used to meet the claims and obligations that will arise as the number of retired people continues to increase.

Norway has achieved surprisingly good results in many areas and, given its modest population, nobody can complain about the country's contribution to the world community. With only 0.007 per cent of the global population, Norway accounts for well above one per cent of world trade and almost five per cent of its maritime transport.

Norwegians are often found in the front rank of many sports. This is particularly true for winter sports, of course, and Norway has won a large share of medals at the winter Olympics over the years.

The Norwegians have also made their mark in international development and as peace brokers. That is perhaps not so surprising in the country responsible for the most prestigious of all awards, the Nobel Peace Prize. This book seeks to present Norwegian industry at the end of a century that has transformed Norway from a poverty-stricken backwater to a prosperous modern community, with the whole world as its market and partner.

STRUGGLING WITH NATURE

Technical progress during our century has been particularly important in a country with Norway's rugged climate and difficult terrain. Norwegian history reflects the eternal struggle of its people with natural forces. This finds expression, for instance, in the old saying that has been borne painfully home to many people along the coast: the sea gives and the sea takes away.

Developments in communications have revolutionised life for most Norwegians. A network of airports, roads driven through and beneath the mountains, and bridges spanning sounds and fjords ties together communities that were previously isolated. Better weather forecasts and well-developed rescue services make life safer both at sea and on land.

From the earliest times, the sea has been a natural highway for people living along Norway's lengthy coast. Crossing the mountains and the precipitous valley sides was almost impossible. Nor were suitable roads easy to build when the motor car appeared at the beginning of the century. But narrow, winding highways eventually replaced the sea routes. Motorists were and are dependent on ferries, but an extensive bridge-building programme has eliminated such vessels on the main routes. Modern snow clearance equipment and tunnels also make it possible to keep the principal mountain crossings open during the winter.

The Vikings developed their legendary longships more than a thousand years ago to carry them along their own shores and across the seas to foreign parts. Norway's mariners later became carriers to the world, bearing the Norwegian flag over the seven seas and making the country one of the world's major shipping nations. More than 1 300 Norwegian merchant vessels currently ply the seas without ever calling at a port in Norway.

Shipping is admittedly less important for the country than it used to be, but almost a quarter of Norway's non-oil exports still relate to the maritime sector.

The number of Norwegian seafarers has declined considerably over recent decades, and they are outnumbered on the country's ships today by Filipinos. However, Norway's maritime industries also include shipyards, production of ship's gear and the expertise needed to operate a merchant fleet. These activities still provide the equivalent of 70 000 full-time jobs for Norwegians.

Winding way. From the Seljestadjuvet gorge on the route between Telemark and Hardanger. New highways through the mountains are replacing the narrow roads that wind up the valley sides.

Bridging the gaps. Road-building in Norway is an expensive business, with the terrain presenting constant challenges to the highway engineer. Twenty-five of the world's 100 longest road tunnels lie in Norway, and the highway network also includes 17 000 bridges. When the Skamsund Bridge in Nord-Trøndelag opened in 1991, it ranked as the world's longest cable-stayed span.

In-depth skills. Constructing penstock tunnels and underground hydropower stations has also helped to give Norwegians special skills in rock blasting. A growing number of road tunnels are replacing long diversions around fjords and mountains, dramatically reducing journey times. With some justice, it has been claimed that the new highways deprive tourists of a chance to enjoy unique scenery in the Norwegian mountains. The scene on the right from the Romsdal Fjord in western Norway typifies the trend. An old road winding along the shore, which was vulnerable to landslides, is being replaced by a secure route beneath the mountains.

Snow trouble. Keeping open the high mountain crossings during the winter is no easy business, even with modern clearing equipment.

Taking the train. The Bergen Railway between Norway's two largest cities, Oslo and Bergen, offers travellers more than an ordinary train journey. From their compartments, they are presented with all the contrasts of the Norwegian landscape. Those who depart from Oslo pass up forested eastern valleys, across the high mountains of the Hardangervidda National Park and down to the western fjord country.

When the 470-kilometre section through the mountains was opened in 1909 after a 15-year construction period, it represented a breakthrough for Norwegian engineering expertise. People today fly between the two cities in just over 30 minutes, but many Norwegians and most foreigners still prefer to spend six-seven hours on the train to experience Norway's mountain scenery.

The train is seen here passing the Hardangervidda National Park on a sunny winter's day.

Tied together (following pages). The sea remains the natural highway for many people living in Norway's island realm, but more and more of these communities are being linked to the mainland by bridge. One example is Henningsvær, a charming and historic fishing village in the northern Lofoten islands. The famous winter Lofoten fishery has been the largest seasonal event for Norwegian fishing people for almost a thousand years.

Faithless servant. The Vikings waited until the spring brought calm weather and long, light nights before setting out on their adventurous voyages more than a millennium ago. Modern equipment and weather forecasting have reduced mishaps along the Norwegian coast, but it will never be possible to avoid all accidents. The picture to the left shows a rescue operation on a stormy autumn day.

Unforgettable cruise. The Coastal Express has operated daily sailings – summer and winter, whatever the weather – between Bergen and northern Norway since 1893. Before air travel, this service bound communities along the coast together. It has now become one of Norway's tourist attractions. The 11-day round trip from Bergen to Kirkenes and back passes some of the country's finest sights, and a cruise on the Coastal Express has become one of the major experiences in European tourism. A modern Coastal Express ship takes a diversion into the Troll Fjord (left).

Flying cat. Almost 40 years have passed since the first high-speed craft revolutionised passenger traffic in Norway. Such craft are also being used for ferry routes to other countries. Kværner Fjellstrand delivers about 20 fast catamarans – FlyingCats – every year from its yards in Norway and Singapore (above and left). These craft are designed for 250-400 passengers, depending on the route to be served.

Flag carrier. Wilh Wilhelmsen's network of shipping lines has made the Norwegian flag familiar world-wide. This Oslo company's ships have carried goods to and from "down under" since its line to Australia was instituted a century ago. Wilhelmsen's Toba is seen on the left passing under Sydney's famous Harbour Bridge during the voyage that marked the line's centenary. The vessel takes 135 days to complete each round-the-world journey.

Modern roll-on, roll-off carriers have substantial capacity. In earlier times, a cargo liner usually loaded 10 000 tonnes in 10-12 different ports. Today's carriers can take on the same volume of goods in one port over a few hours, and are actually able to carry 30-40 000 tonnes. Vehicles of all types are driven on board. An X2000 high-speed railway carriage destined for Australia is loaded on m/s Taiko (top), while new cars from the Far East drive ashore in Europe (above).

Luxury afloat. Little about today's cruise palaces recalls the liners that initiated the cruising business just over a century ago by carrying passengers from Britain to Norway's fjords. When Norwegian shipowners began to offer Caribbean cruises in 1967, they opened a new chapter in the history of holidays at sea. Cruising is now an industry. The biggest luxury liners, accommodating 2 300 passengers, operate mainly in the Caribbean during the winter. But more northerly waters are their most important summer destination.

Two Norwegian companies are among the biggest cruise operators, although only the 10 liners run by Royal Caribbean Cruise Lines fly the national flag. RCCL is the world's second largest cruise specialist, and is adding four more ships to its fleet over the next two years – allowing it to carry 24 700 passengers simultaneously.

DOWN ON THE SEABED

Exploration for oil began off Norway in the second half of the 1960s, but initially yielded such disappointing results that the oil companies began turning their backs on the Norwegian continental shelf. Phillips was the only operator that had not completed its drilling programme in these waters by late autumn 1969. However, the final well proved the winner. The Ekofisk field was discovered on 23 December 1969, and marked the start of an oil adventure that was to have sweeping effects on Norwegian society.

A difficult climate and deep water posed major technical challenges for oil and gas production on Norway's continental shelf. Calling for solutions at the limits of the technologically possible, these problems were overcome with the development of new methods and equipment. This commitment has made Norway one of Europe's principal suppliers of petroleum products.

Thirty-one of the 33 producing Norwegian fields are in the North Sea. Exploration further north is being intensified, with new licences laying the basis for an extensive and stable drilling programme.

Norway's oil and gas resources are much further from being exhausted than many have feared. About 17 per cent of known reserves had been produced in spring 1996, and calculations suggest that 70 per cent of the original resources will still be underground in 2005. Since output started in 1970, known reserves have increased far more than the pace of production thanks to additional discoveries and increases in the recovery factor – in other words, the amount of oil or gas in a field that can actually be brought up. Norway will be able to sustain its present rate of oil production for another 16 years, while gas output could stay at today's level for 108 years. After oil production peaks in 2000, the country will increasingly become a gas supplier. Its gas production is set to double over the next decade.

A total of NOK 550 billion had been invested in Norwegian offshore operations up to 1996. A third of the country's export earnings and 10 per cent of government revenues come from the petroleum sector. Annual offshore income accruing to the authorities is set to triple from NOK 25 billion in 1994 to NOK 70-80 billion in 2000. This reflects not only the rise in gas production but also cuts in development and operating spending as a result of technological advances.

Role change (left). Offshore operations in the North Sea appeared like manna from heaven to Norway's shipyards during the international shipping crisis of the 1970s. They quickly turned to this market, developing major solutions for the industry. These include new types of rig, the Condeep concrete production platforms and modern supply ships. The Ulstein group in western Norway was one of the companies which made a heavy commitment to the offshore market. The picture on the left is from Ulstein Verft.

Fine finds (following pages). Most Norwegian offshore fields derive their names from Norse mythology or the nation's history. In its day, the Oseberg ship grave south of Oslo yielded some of the biggest treasures ever discovered from Norway's Viking past. The vessel and other objects from this find can be admired today at the Viking Ship Museum in Oslo. But Oseberg has also given its name to one of the biggest oil fields in the Norwegian North Sea, where the weather can occasionally be dramatic.

Giant challenge. Troll is one of the biggest offshore gas fields ever found, and its development has ranked as the world's largest energy project. It also represents the most demanding challenge faced in these waters so far. A total of NOK 120 billion has been invested in platforms, pipelines, terminals and receiving facilities in Germany and Belgium. Contracts won by Norwegian industry from this development account for 85 per cent of the value of engineering work, 75 per cent of the platform and 61 per cent of the land plant.

Developing Troll has required installations unmatched in human history, including the impressive gas production platform. With a displacement of one million tonnes, this 472-metre-high colossus is pictured on the left in idyllic surroundings before being towed to the field in May 1995. The five-day voyage was completed without incident.

Norway's Aker group built the concrete gravity base structure as well as the topsides with living quarters and drilling equipment. Norske Shell was responsible for the Troll gas development, while Statoil took over as production operator in summer 1996.

Sales agreements covering Troll gas deliveries for the next 25-30 years have been signed with a consortium of European buyers. Worth NOK 700 billion, these contracts will make Norway a leading supplier of gas to continental Europe well into the next century.

Northern pioneer. All Norwegian oil production flowed from the North Sea until 1994, when Draugen came on stream in the Norwegian Sea. Output from this field is loaded into special tankers (above) and shipped to the crude oil terminal at Mongstad near Bergen.

Deep down. The Troll A platform closed a chapter in North Sea history, and will probably be the last giant built for these waters. Until now, Condeep concrete platforms have played a key role in the rough seas off Norway's shores and represent a major triumph for Norwegian engineering skills.

However, ever-increasing water depths made these facilities so costly that new answers had to be found. Production ships and remotely-operated installations on the seabed will be preferred for future developments.

The little Tordis field in the North Sea illustrates what this new technology involves. Ringed by three of the largest Norwegian fields – Statfjord, Gullfaks and Snorre – this discovery could only be produced profitably by combining new subsea technology with existing infrastructure. Development costs on Tordis are so low that it ranks as one of the most profitable Norwegian fields, breaking even at an oil price of USD 8 per barrel.

Subsea centre. A seabed manifold is the hub for control signals, oil production and water injection, and serves as the central unit in subsea production. As the pictures above and right show, these installations have impressive dimensions. This 2 500-tonne steel structure forms the underwater centre on the Snorre field. Hinged covers make it possible to service the valves with mini-submarines. The manifold was installed in May 1992.

Broad involvement. Norwegian industry is heavily involved in offshore deliveries, and 171 companies in Norway each supplied equipment worth more than NOK 3 million to the Troll Gas project. Control modules (left) are installed at Kongsberg Offshore.

due to begin operating at Tjeldbergodden in mid-Norway during April 1997, will process gas from the Heidrun field in the Norwegian Sea.

Two gas-fired power stations are also planned to generate electricity for export. This scheme is strongly opposed by environmentalists. Norwegians have generally shown little enthusiasm for developing industries to process their offshore resources, preferring to see the oil or gas exported.

Submarine energy. As a leading expert on submarine power cables, Alcatel Norge has won major contracts all over the world. The company has laid 1 300 underwater cables in Norway and is naturally also involved offshore. The submarine power line from Troll A to the Kollsnes terminal was laid (below) by an Alcatel ship. Unlike other offshore installations, this platform is powered from the Norwegian grid rather than generating its own electricity. Fibre-optic communication and control cables allow the unit to be operated from land.

Better and cheaper. Norway's offshore development costs have been reduced by 30-50 per cent over the past few years. Greater standardisation has cut planning and construction times, while new technology makes it possible to use cheaper solutions such as subsea satellites and horizontal drilling. With its maritime traditions, it is hardly surprising that Norway has taken a lead in using production ships. Petrojarl 1 (left) began operating in the 1980s.

A fleet of production vessels is now under construction at various yards around the world, and will increasingly be preferred to fixed platforms. Off Norway, such ships are due to produce oil from fields like Balder, Norne, Njord, Åsgard and Varg. Semisubmersible platforms will also be considered as production moves into ever deeper water. The new exploration areas in the Norwegian and Barents Seas are as deep as 1 400 metres. Innovative solutions will be needed to exploit possible discoveries in such depths.

Processing petroleum. Offshore operations have not yielded any major petrochemical developments in Norway, apart from the Bamble complex (above) south of Oslo that was built in the 1970s. Various refineries also base most of their production on feedstock from the North Sea.

The biggest land-based facilities are otherwise the gas treatment plants at Kårstø north of Stavanger and Kollsnes near Bergen. One of the world's largest methanol plants,

THANKS FOR RAINY DAYS

Nobody talks as often or as much about the weather as Norwegians, and few have such good grounds to complain about the climate than people in western and northern Norway. Bergen, the biggest city on the west coast, is the true home of the umbrella. Moist masses of air flow in from the Atlantic and pour cascades of water over coasts and mountains to fill more than 200 000 highland lakes and the network of rivers and streams that run from them. Apart from enlivening the landscape, this flow has been tamed on its way to the sea and converted into cheap, clean and renewable energy.

Hydropower accounts for a larger share of energy consumption in Norway than in other countries, and has played a key role in transforming this nation into a modern industrial community. The country currently has some 600 hydropower stations, meeting most energy needs for both industry and households.

Some of Norway's key export products can be regarded as processed energy, and the country ranks as a major supplier of important electro-metals. Its energy resources laid the basis for several of the biggest Norwegian manufacturing firms. The largest of them all, Norsk Hydro, was founded in 1905 to use hydropower in making fertiliser. Although the company remains one of the world's leading producers of this product, its output is based today on oil and gas. On the other hand, all Hydro's production of light metals continues to rely on hydro-electricity.

Developing Norway's hydropower resources has called for engineering skills of the highest order. The largest Norwegian underground power stations are big enough to accommodate homes for 2 000 people. Experience from building such facilities has been applied to excavating rock caverns for storage and sports arenas as well as tunnels both at home and abroad. Similarly, power station equipment, electro-smelting technology and products for the metallurgical industry have become Norwegian specialities with a world market.

Using hydropower is fully in line with modern environmentalist attitudes. But the demands of nature conservation make it increasingly difficult to develop Norway's remaining rivers. So modernising existing facilities rather than further disruption of the natural environment will be important for expanding energy production.

Tight grid. Hydropower stations large and small are tied together by a Norwegian national grid with links to Sweden and Denmark. A surplus of hydro-electricity in Norway can be sent to these neighbours in exchange for power from them at times when low precipitation reduces Norwegian water supplies.

Between heaven and earth. Installing electricity transmission cables across mountains and fjords looks a hazardous business. On the following pages, a construction worker sways high above the Eid Fjord in Hardanger on the west coast.

Dream became reality. More than 4 500 kilometres of tunnels have been driven beneath Norway's mountains. Some are for roads, railways, telecommunications, defence purposes and water supply, but the majority – extending 3 500 kilometres – relate to major hydropower developments over the past 50 years.

Ulla-Førre north-east of Stavanger is northern Europe's largest hydropower project, producing 1 240 MW of electricity in all. This scheme realised an old dream, but the developers had to wait until the 1970s for technology that permitted work to proceed in an inaccessible mountain region.

Different interests also had to be weighed against each other during the development. Nature conservation makes important demands on hydropower projects today, but Ulla-Førre was eventually approved and has long been in operation. Water from 20 reservoirs and 40 rivers is guided to the power stations through 100 kilometres of tunnel. The Ulla-Førre system of dams (above) is one of the largest in the world.

Four tracks. They say four tracks run through Norwegian history – the wake of ships, the furrow of the plough across fields, ski trails through the forest and the transmission lines (right) that carry hydropower to consumers.

Ice scheme. The latest power project in Norway is the development of Svartisen, the country's second largest glacier, which lies close to the Arctic Circle. Although this scheme extends across four local authorities, only a small part of the glacier is affected and the region's scenic attractions will remain unblemished. A stream of tourist liners sails along the Norwegian coast during the summer. Most call at Engabreen, a Svartisen arm that extends almost to the sea.

Rock-filled. The Storglomvass dam, part of the Svartisen development, will contain Norway's biggest reservoir. Standing 126 metres high and measuring 800 metres long, it ranks as the world's largest rock-fill dam. The actual power station will be in a rock cavern 900 metres below ground. State-owned developer Statsbygg, which

owns 58 power stations in Norway, is pursuing the project.

Since 1978, dams for Norwegian power stations have featured an impervious asphalt core running from bottom to top that is installed (top left) by modern machines able to work in all kinds of weather. The core in Storglomvass is 90 centimetres wide at its base, narrowing to 50 centimetres at the top. Korsbrekke og Lorck, part of the Veidekke group, is responsible for the core in this dam.

Power products. Power station equipment has become a Norwegian speciality. Turbines produced by Kværner Energy (above) are among the products from Norway that have found a place in hydropower projects worldwide in recent years.

Norway's biggest-ever hydropower generator (below left), with an output of 410 MVA, has been delivered by ABB to the Svartisen project.

Beneficial by-products. Norway ranks as one of the world's leading producers of metals, which account for a quarter of its non-oil commodity exports. Production is primarily based on hydropower. All industrial operations have environmental consequences, but new processes and investment in clean-up measures at the smelters over the past few decades have cut emissions of fumes and other pollutants by as much as 80 per cent.

The need to reduce emissions also prompted a search for ways of utilising waste products more effectively. Materials that once polluted the landscape around smelting plants have become useful by-products. Two examples are the ferro-silicon produced by Elkem as a strength additive for concrete and Norzink's use of zinc waste in paint. Elkem is also a technical pioneer in the smelting sector, with its products installed world-wide. These scenes are from Elkem Fiskaa at Kristiansand in southern Norway.

Green metal. Aluminium is an environment-friendly product. Not only is more than half the world's output of this metal based on hydropower, but resmelting also demands little energy and has no impact on its properties. Ninety per cent of the aluminium used in the transport sector can be sorted out and re-used for the same purpose. Large amounts of energy are needed to produce the metal, but production methods developed over the past 20 years have cut power requirements by 15 per cent. At the same time, new closed furnaces reduce earlier pollution problems in their immediate vicinity. Heat losses in process industries have been cut by re-using this energy or applying it to warm commercial buildings and homes.

Hydro Aluminium has an annual capacity of 700 000 tonnes of unwrought aluminium, produced exclusively with hydropower. The company also recycles 110 000 tonnes of the metal per year. It operates 38 companies and employs 6 000 people. Hydro turns about half of the unwrought aluminium it produces into extrusions for products with various degrees of finish, building systems, automotive components, rolled and coated products and specialised items such as air freight containers, electrical cabinets, lorry bodies and packaging.

Extrusion ingots are a principal product at the Karmøy plant north of Stavanger (top).

Lighter cars. As Europe's largest producer of aluminium and magnesium, Norway has become an important supplier to European car-makers increasingly concerned with producing light and environment-friendly vehicles.

Norsk Hydro, one of the many Norwegian manufacturers of automotive components, has tested unusually robust aluminium chassis frames (far left). The group also delivers wheel rims in this metal for a number of car makes, including Opel, Audi, BMW, Saab and Volvo. Development of such rims at Fundo in western Norway is pictured above.

But component deliveries are not restricted to light metals. Norway ranks, for instance, as a major supplier of plastic petrol tanks (left).

UNDERGROUND TREASURES

It should come as no surprise to learn that mining is one of the oldest industries in a mountain nation like Norway. But extracting minerals and ores has never been very significant for the Norwegian economy. Deposits are small by international standards, and most mining ventures have ended in financial collapse. The history of Norway's mining industry is full of tales of poverty and deprivation, because few businesses experience such variations in demand and prices over time. These fluctuations cause particular difficulties for mining communities, which are usually isolated and lack other sources of jobs when the mines fail.

Most ore discoveries in Norway have been made accidentally by hunters, fishing folk and reindeer herders, who virtually stumbled over a deposit during their wanderings in the desolate mountains. Finds seldom resulted from systematic exploration, and a complete survey of Norwegian ore reserves has still to made. So dreams of striking it rich persist in many parts of the country.

Mines opened in the 17th and 18th centuries are only history now, but the copper town of Røros in east-central Norway remains a living memorial to a vanished era. This community is one of four Norwegian sites on Unesco's World Heritage list, along with the Bryggen wharf in Bergen, Norway's oldest stave church at Urnes and the Alta rock carvings in the far north.

Kongsberg west of Oslo is another town built on mining. Its silver mines were once the country's biggest industrial operation and financed many wars against Sweden when Norway was part of Denmark. With the mines long closed, Kongsberg has become a centre for technological research and production.

A mining community with problems is Kirkenes on the border with Russia, which was founded on the extraction and processing of iron ore. Declining profitability created many headaches for the authorities, not only because few other jobs were available locally but also because settlement had to be maintained in the regions bordering the Soviet Union during the Cold War. Mining is now closing down, and efforts are being made to attract new industries.

Norway's biggest ore reserves today are Titania's ilmenite deposits at the Jøssing Fjord on the south-west coast, which yield about three million tonnes per year.

Natural art. The picture on the left has not been created by some great artist, but by nature itself. This rare Blue Pearl granite contains blue crystals and is quarried in the Larvik area south of Oslo. Applications include interior and exterior cladding for buildings in many countries. Treschow Fritzøe has exported stone from its own quarries since 1970, but an involvement in Norwegian industry dating as far back as 1540 makes this the country's oldest company.

Mystery mountains. Some of the highlands that cover two-thirds of Norway, like Buerdalen in Hardanger (following pages), look mysterious and inaccessible.

Good as gold. The nepheline syenite found on Stjernøy in the far northern county of Finnmark (preceding pages) is worth its weight in gold to North Cape Minerals. This company supplies glass and china manufacturers in many countries from the island, which lies almost 1 000 kilometres above the Arctic Circle. A mine located virtually on the roof of world, a hour by boat from its nearest neighbours, might be expected to face many handicaps – including a long way to market. Stjernøy admittedly lies off the beaten track, but transport to the mine's principal customers in Europe is no problem. Most mines around the world depend on long and expensive overland transport, but the island has a first-class

harbour. Despite its northerly location, this is ice-free all year.

Darkness prevails almost around the clock in winter. The mine is pictured here on a January noon, when the sun fails to rise above the horizon and a month-long twilight shrouds the landscape during the day.

Cold coal. Norway does not end at the North Cape. On the edge of the Arctic Ocean lie the Svalbard islands, which derive their collective name from the Viking term for "cold coast country". And that name is apt. Snow and ice cover part of the land, while drift ice fills the chill seas around it. Spread across 700 kilometres from north to south, these islands

contain the world's northernmost permanent human settlements. They used to be cut off during the winter months, but daily flights now maintain contact with the rest of Norway all year round.

Norway consumes little coal, but mines for this fuel still provide a living for most of the 3 000 residents in Svalbard. Working conditions in the galleries are far from comfortable, as the pictures on this page show, but a long and sad series of accidents in the first decades after the Second World War has fortunately been replaced by an even longer period without major incidents.

ARCHITECTURE FOR A NEW AGE

Glacial gallery. The Norwegian Museum of Glaciology at Fjærland in western Norway is one of architect Sverre Fehn's exciting museum buildings. It stands like a grey boulder carried by the ice, almost resembling a glacier itself. Concrete is the principal material, and the slanting walls merge naturally into the surrounding mountainsides. This scene from the museum shows how Fehn uses wood as both construction material and decorative element.

Wood has always been an important building material in Norway, and the roughly 800 stave churches constructed around the country during the Middle Ages represent its greatest contribution to European culture. Thirty-one of these buildings have survived, putting them among the world's oldest timber structures still in use. The stave church and the Viking long ship are monuments to Norway's rich past, with decorations that reveal handicraft skills of a high order. Copies of these vessels and churches have been built in recent years, so that old traditions live on more than a millennium after the ancestors of today's Norwegians created masterpieces with their simple tools.

Wood remains the dominant material for detached homes and holiday cabins in Norway. Leading architects also make extensive use of timber in large structures. Wide ceilings supported by laminated beams have become a characteristic feature of many Norwegian buildings, such as the stadiums constructed for the Olympic winter games at Lillehammer north of Oslo in 1994.

In many respects, Norwegians have overtaken the other Nordic countries that used to lead the way in Scandinavian architecture. With unconventional designs and new use of materials, they have freed themselves from old traditions and won prestigious international awards.

Our age demands architecture with a human dimension, and Norway's architects appear to have succeeded in emphasising this aspect in new solutions for office buildings. The present trend towards decentralised organisations permits designs that eliminate or lower boundaries between departments while providing space for communication and more freedom of movement for each employee. Several office or administration buildings constructed in Norway during recent years adopt an open form, with large central atria that feature extensive use of glass and space for corridors, stairways and diagonal bridges linking floors and wings. Staff canteens often look more like street cafes on the continental European model.

Norwegian families spend a lot of time indoors, and invest more of their income in home and furnishings than people in many other countries. The prosperity achieved by many Norwegians over the past few generations, combined with an ever stronger ecological awareness, presents Norwegian architects with new challenges.

Human proportions. No other architect in Norway can match Sverre Fehn's international standing. Since winning the competition to design Norway's pavilion at the 1958 World Exposition in Brussels, he has been a pioneer in Norwegian architecture. He is pictured above outside the Kjell Aukrust Centre at Alvdal in eastern Norway. Few artists live to see a museum dedicated to their work, but that honour has befallen humorist and cartoonist Aukrust. This building also typifies Fehn's choice of materials.

Modern architecture with a more human expression is how this Norwegian's work has been described. His work includes the privately-owned Villa Busk (right), built in 1990 and already subject to a conservation order. Standing on a small hill by the coast, this private residence achieves an unusual interaction between the natural setting and materials such as concrete, wood, glass and slate.

Fehn's most recent international success was his victory in the competition for the new Royal Theatre in Copenhagen, which is due to be completed in 2000. He also has other major museum assignments in Norway.

On holy ground. Norway's most modern library has been built in its oldest city, Tønsberg, directly on the ruins of St Olav's monastery. Consecrated in 1180, these former cloisters helped to inspire the architectural form of the library and the choice of building materials. The Lunde & Løvseth firm of architects won the competition for this project in 1988, and the building was completed in 1992. Large sheets of laminated glass are held in a steel structure inspired by trees. Archaeological finds made on the site are incorporated into the library.

Concrete kudos. It would be impossible to imagine a modern community without concrete, and this material finds a variety of applications in Norway – offshore platforms, buildings of all kinds, roads and bridges. But concrete can also be used as a decorative element in its own right. Norway's concrete industry awards an annual prize to a structure that makes the best use of this material's qualities. The 1995 accolade went to ØKAW Arkitekter for a laboratory building commissioned by state-owned Statsbygg for three health institutions. Measuring 110 metres long, the building (detail, left) features prominent pairs of columns and facade beams in prefabricated concrete.

ØKAW has also won the concrete award once before, for its work on the Olympic ski jumping and ceremony arenas at Lillehammer.

Free flight. Concrete is a malleable material that can also be cast into animals and other figures. The playful capercaillie (below) in Hønefoss north of Oslo shows how artworks can be created in concrete.

Subterranean stadium (preceding pages). The Olympic Cavern Hall at Gjøvik in eastern Norway is the largest underground arena ever built, and can seat more than 6 000 people when rigged for ice hockey. This stadium attracted more attention from international construction experts than any other installation built for the 1994 winter Olympics. It provides visible evidence of Norwegian rock blasting skills and shows how underground caverns can be incorporated into city centres that have little spare space. Originally built to stage ice hockey games, this facility is also well-suited for conferences, concerts and other events.

Forward-looking. Statoil's new Research Centre in Trondheim (left) also provides advanced training for researchers in the state oil company. Laboratories, workshops and offices occupy two wings that face the Trondheim Fjord and are linked by a large glass vestibule. A key requirement for the design by Per Knudsen Arkitektkontor was to preserve the attractive fjordside landscape.

Popular playground. Architect Niels Torp has handled major assignments both at home and abroad. In Oslo, his name is closely linked with one of the most eye-catching projects of recent decades in the Norwegian capital – the conversion of a former shipyard into the Aker Brygge complex of restaurants, shops, offices and homes. This site has always stood at the centre of Oslo, but the yard was a barrier between city and sea. Its redevelopment has restored the close contact between the pulsating downtown area and the harbour basin.

Aker Brygge represents the new Oslo that has emerged over the past few decades, to earn a reputation as northern Europe's most lively and youthful metropolis. The charming harbour frontage created right in front of the City Hall has become a major attraction for both locals and visitors.

Abroad, Torp has won competitions to design new head offices for two of Europe's largest airlines – Scandinavian Airline System (SAS) and British Airways. The SAS premises in Stockholm have been described as lying neither in the country nor in the city. It represents a new type of office building featuring covered glass surfaces and open-plan offices, intermixed with areas of parkland. This building has long been occupied, but BA's new headquarters in London is under construction.

Prestige project. One of the most startling victories won internationally by Norwegian architects in recent years is the Snøhetta company's design for a new national library at Alexandria in Egypt (above).

This building aims to restore the memory of the largest library in the ancient world, founded by Alexander the Great more than 2 000 years ago. Five hundred architects from all over the world competed for this prestigious job.

Six years after Snøhetta's concept took first prize, construction work is in full swing and the building should be inaugurated in 1999. The computer revolution changed all the old library concepts during the design phase, but this has been taken into account while retaining the original overall form. The sloping roof of the actual library slices through the ground and into the water, giving it a boat-like appearance. Half the building is below ground level, providing the books with a protected environment and a favourable climate. Several furniture manufacturers in Norway are designing special products for the library, with support from the Norwegian authorities.

Past under glass. Wind, frost and damp erode many historic monuments, and experts accordingly want to find ways of conserving the national heritage for future generations. The cathedral ruins at Hamar north of Oslo have been among the threatened memorials. This building was one of the finest churches in Norway until the Swedes blew it up in 1750. Proposals by Lund & Slaatto, which won a 1987 competition to enclose the ruins on the shores of Lake Mjøsa, have since been controversial. The architects want to raise a 22-metre-high vault in glass and aluminium like a cathedral over the remains. A constant temperature and humidity can be maintained internally. The supporting structure leaves the ruins highly visible.

Travel temple. A new airport for Oslo has been under discussion for 30 years, and 13 Norwegian communications ministers have worked on the subject.

This facility will finally be opened on 4 October 1998 at Gardermoen just over 40 kilometres north of the capital. Including Norway's first high-speed rail link, the project is costed at about NOK 20 million. The new train service will carry passengers between central Oslo and Gardermoen in 19 minutes.

Two parallel runways are being constructed at the airport, while the terminal building will feature the world's largest laminated timber ceiling beams. These come from Moelven Industrier, which also delivered the massive wooden structures for the Olympic stadiums in Hamar and Lillehammer.

DESIGN LENGTHENS LIFE

Scandinavian design is functional and aesthetic in its forms and choice of materials. It has influenced several generations of architects, furniture and fashion designers and craft workers. Although always rooted in the Scandinavian ethos, modern Norwegian design has gained a more distinctively national character in recent years.

Naturally enough, most people associate design with furniture, furnishings, textiles and artware. However, industrial design sets its stamp on every part of our daily lives – not only shaping the objects that surround us at home and work, but also playing an ever-bigger role in the process from idea to finished product.

The growing importance of design is not accidental. An age of abundance has prompted a more systematic approach to product appearance, functionality and user-friendliness. Form and function must be viewed together. Design also offers a tool for enhancing quality, safeguarding the environment and achieving simpler and more rational production processes that can reduce prices.

Many companies have found that an attractive appearance gives added value, and that good looks combined with user-friendliness help to boost sales. Product lifetimes are getting steadily shorter, but good design has often extended the life of an artifact and allowed it to survive changing fashions.

The Norwegian Design Council's Classic Prize is awarded annually to a design product that has maintained its market position for many years. Some of the biggest successes from Norway's furniture industry are among the winners. Chairs like the Siesta, the Stressless and the Tripp Trapp have been best-sellers for more than 20 years, and remain a key factor in Norwegian furniture exports.

A recent research report on five Norwegian companies concluded that professional industrial design has made a significant contribution to sales results. Firms covered by the study included Tomra, a specialist in automated handling of returnable bottles which quadrupled sales from 1988 to 1994. Furniture-make Håg, also covered, boosted profits sevenfold in 1994. And Hamax, which makes sports and leisure equipment, noted a 133 per cent rise in sales after introducing a new child seat for bicycles in 1993 that also won an award for good design.

Adornment to art. Tone Vigeland has been a standard-bearer for Norwegian art jewellery for many years. This lovely and original necklace can be seen in the Cooper-Hewitt National Design Museum of the Smithsonian Institution in New York.

Olympic winner. Norwegian design achieved a kind of national breakthrough during the winter Olympics at Lillehammer in 1994. No single event has ever aroused such interest in design among the general public in Norway. A special programme highlighted domestic values in design, architecture, the environment and culture. Everyone present at the games or who watched them on TV was struck by the unified image achieved for the event, from stadiums and decorations to signs, tickets, medals and the many products produced on licence. The design programme emphasised national individuality and traditions, while expressing joy and personal fulfilment in line with Olympic ideals.

The pictograms proved the most eye-catching element in the programme. Thousands of years ago, Norway's earliest artists carved figures in the rock – including a skier. This image was allied with today's artistry to create a visual symbol, an ingenious expression of the Olympic links between ancient and modern times. These pictograms at-

tracted great attention and conveyed their message in a clear fashion. The programme won the Scandinavian design prize for 1994.

Pictured here are the colourful opening ceremony at Lillehammer (above) and medals carrying the pictograms (right).

Dale Fabrikker and rugs in pure lamb's wool (below) from Berger, which exports 50 per cent of its production.

Ultra-Norwegian. No other product is so closely associated with Norway than the knitted pullover. Few foreigners return from a Norwegian holiday minus one of these garments, with its special pattern and combination of colours. Knitting has old traditions, and many women in rural areas still knit pullovers and other garments for domestic shops or for export.

Norwegian wool is very suitable for the chunky and sturdy products so characteristic of knitwear from Norway. Roughly a quarter of the sheep in Norway are short-tailed spelsau. This old national breed yields the famous spelsau wool, which is highly popular for hand-kitted garments, tapestries and artworks.

The pictures on this page present knitwear fashions (above and above right) from

Glass skills. Art glass has old traditions in Norway, with the finest objects made at Nøstetangen in the second half of the 18th century. These pieces command fantastic prices when they occasionally appear at international auctions. Norwegian glassmaking skills live on in both industrial and art products.

A set of Olympic tableware (left) was produced by Hadeland Glassverk for the 1994 games, one of the many licensed products that benefitted both organiser and manufacturer.

Autumn flavour. Rowan berries are sour and hang high, people say. But they form an essential ingredient, both as a table decoration and as a preserve, when meats from the autumn hunt are served. And they are used (left) in the "hunter's sup" drink. The glasses are made by Hilde L Isaksen at Glasshytta in Kragerø south of Oslo.

Spring drink. Hand-blown glasses from Glasshytta Hegg (below) contain concentrated birch sap, which imparts a refined sweet flavour when mixed with aquavit or sparkling wine.

Rustic room. The kitchen has always been the place where people congregate in Norwegian homes. This rustic dining space (above) provides a warm and intimate setting for gatherings of close friends on long evenings. The table is unpretentious, informal and non-traditional, but nevertheless festive, and achieves an exuberant blend of colours and shapes. Table, plate rack and corner cupboard, made by Norwegian Antique Design, are inspired by old models.

Winning designs. The Norwegian Design Council has awarded its annual Good Design Award for industrial products since 1963. These pages present some of the winners.

Hamax won in both 1993 and 1995 for its Discovery series of family products designed for cyclists (right). This mother is out for a ride with her children in patented safety seats, and everyone wears helmets in matching colours.

CompactVision (below) is a future-oriented videophone system. Such solutions are expected to find their primary application in video conferencing, but this could truly be a product for the next century.

Luxo's amusing and functional Heron lamps (bottom) are clearly inspired by the bird. From modest beginnings in 1934, this company has become an international group producing light fittings in many countries.

A log-handler (above) is not something one usually associates with design. But if a single unit sells on its looks, the design costs will have been covered, says Scandlog manufacturer Kaldnes. This device has attracted great international attention in the forest industry.

Turn for the better. It took six years for the inventors of the Mobilix turnable examination table to get this health care product into production. The whole project was on the verge of collapse before an industrial designer succeeded in finding a way out. Mobilix is now in use at hospitals in both Norway and abroad.

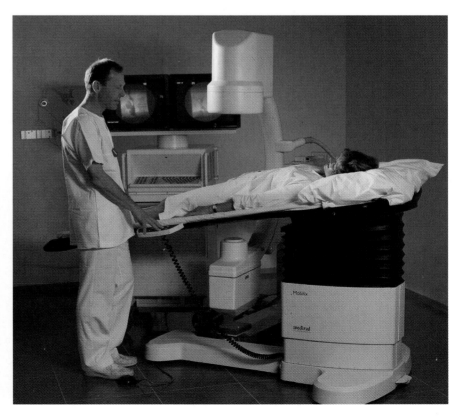

Timeless taste. In an age when product lifetimes are getting ever shorter, this antique stove (left) from Ulefoss Jærnverk is worthy of note as the oldest Norwegian industrial artifact in continuous production. The stove and its panels were designed by Danish sculptor Henrik Bech 230 years ago, and output started in 1766. With its attractive decor derived from Greek mythology, this unit is still delivered to customers in Norway and abroad. The stove remained the main product from the Ulefoss foundry until the second half of this century.

Founded in 1640, Ulefoss Jærnverk is the second oldest industrial company in Norway. Only Treschow Fritzøe in Larvik, which initiated its first sawmill in 1540, dates further back.

All-time best. The Stressless is Norway's biggest-ever furniture success. First presented at an Oslo exhibition in 1971, it was initially intended to give manufacturer Ekornes a more up-market image. The chair had limited success initially in Norway, and only one customer bought it. On the other hand, that buyer was no less a store than Harrods of London.

More than two million Stressless chairs have since been sold, and the design is regarded today more as a seating concept than as a single item of furniture. Countless manufacturers have produced imitations that are claimed to possess all the original's good qualities.

The Stressless name is registered in more than 30 countries. Ranked today as Scandinavia's largest furniture company, Ekornes derives 60 per cent of its revenues from this chair.

Sit with style. Designer Peter Opsvik (above, in one of his Balance chairs) is a name to conjure with in Norway's furniture business today. He has single-handedly put Norwegian furniture design on the map, creating several of the most popular products introduced in recent decades by companies such as Stokke and Håg. These include the Balance seating concept, his Tripp Trapp children's chair and dynamic products for office and home. Opsvik creates furniture intended to vitalise users and to encourage activity and well-being.

Cylindra (right) was originally inspired by wooden herring casks. This series combines artistic expression with

functionality. While Opsvik's other chairs provide opportunities to move the body, Cylindra is intended to encourage thoughts to flow.

Chair cheer. Håg has become one of Europe's largest, most dynamic and most experimental manufacturers of office chairs. Its philosophy is that sitting does not come naturally to humans, although many spend much of their working life seated. People think better when they can move freely, the company believes, and offers solutions that promote motion and varied posture. Håg's factory stands in the former mining town of Røros in eastern Norway. The Capisco (right) seems appropriate for many applications outside the office. Below right is the Håg Scio.

Child classic. Scandinavian's best-selling children's chair, Stokke's Tripp Trapp (below) literally grows with its user. Both seat and footrest can be re-positioned as the child gets bigger. Since its introduction 25 years ago, more than two million Tripp Trapps have been sold. The chair won the Norwegian Design Council's Classic Prize in 1995.

FROM NATURE'S LARDER

Norwegians have been harvesting the seas since the first people moved into the country more than 10 000 years ago. Later, the Vikings took fish on their trading voyages to exchange for other products they needed. Seafood accordingly became Norway's first export product. Handling the sale of fish from northern Norway made Bergen one of the greatest north European cities in the Middle Ages.

Few new industries mean more for Norway than aquaculture. The country offers particularly favourable conditions for fish farming, since the Gulf Stream keeps sea temperatures stable year-round along the entire coast. So the 700 Norwegian fish farms can produce more cheaply and efficiently than their rivals in other countries.

From earliest times, the sea provided an economic basis for Norway's coastal communities. Their fortunes therefore varied with the fish catch. If the fisheries failed, the coastal population always faced problems. Overfishing as a result of efficient new technology made it necessary to impose catch ceilings and quota schemes that allowed stocks to be rebuilt. Norway's fisheries are now enjoying good times, with big catches and high demand in international markets. Experience with strict Norwegian fishing curbs underlines the necessity of regulating fisheries and relating quotas to stocks. But achieving agreement on quotas is not easy in international waters, where different national interests can clash.

Developing Norway's aquaculture business is an adventure that bears comparison with the offshore sector. This industry has created 15 000 new jobs in parts of the country with little basis for other economic activity. Norway produced more salmon than meat in 1995, and this fish has become one of the most important Norwegian export commodities.

All the attention given to fish farming should not cause anyone to think that traditional sea fishing has lost its significance. The inshore fisheries remain the most important source of income for most coastal communities, and Norway has never earned more from this sector than it does today. Hundreds of plants along the entire coast process catches from their immediate waters and help to maintain Norway's strong position in world fish markets.

Medieval methods. Drying and salting were once the most widely-used techniques for conserving fish. Stockfish is still dried in northern Norway by the same methods used in the Middle Ages. As soon as the fish comes ashore, it is hung out on big wooden frames, or hjell, and dries rock-hard in the cool, fresh sea air. A kilogram of stockfish has the same nutritional content as five kilograms of fresh cod.

Fleet foray. Inshore fishing from smaller vessels, like those setting out here, has provided many Norwegian coastal communities with their livelihood down the ages.

Red catch. After farmed salmon, cod is the most important fish in the Norwegian economy. But a variety of other species caught off Norway are also exported, such as these flavourful redfish (above).

Salted speciality. Unlike stockfish, codfish is salted before being dried. Originally spread out to dry on the rocks along the coast, this product is now prepared in modern drying plants. Ålesund on the west coast is not only the centre for one of Norway's most industrious manufacturing regions, but also serves as the country's

largest port for fish exports. Two 10-year-olds (left) display a first-class piece of codfish on the Ålesund waterfront. Now measuring a metre long and weighing nine kilograms, this product weighed 40-45 kilograms when it swam in the sea.

Cheating camera. The Norwegian fishing fleet totals 8 000 vessels, mainly small craft. But the 300 largest units account for 65 per cent of the catch and are the most profitable. Fishing crews must be prepared for winds and high seas, but modern weather forecasting and better equipment make their lives less risky than in the open boats of olden times. They seldom experience conditions as threatening as those that appear to face Røstværing in this picture from the Røst Sea off Lofoten. But things look worse than they are as the boat disappears into the trough of a wave. A third of all stockfish sold in Italy comes from the little island of Røst.

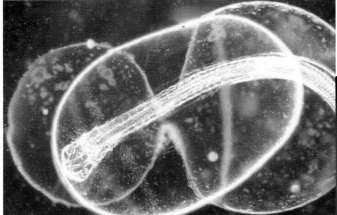

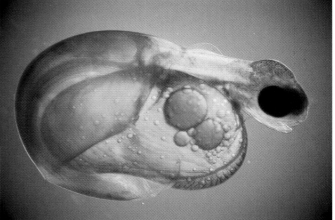

Emergent life. Fish breeding has made great strides in the aquaculture sector. These unique pictures show a halibut (left) and a salmon (below) emerging from their eggs.

Less stress, better taste. When salmon get stressed, they consume body substances that otherwise help to give them the right flavour. So the way these fish spend their final hours, including conditions in the boat carrying them to slaughter, may affect their quality. Stress responses can be measured directly from chemical reactions in the flesh. A young salmon is prepared (above) for testing at Sintef Unimed. This facility forms part of Sintef, Norway's largest research organisation.

Seaward shift. The first Norwegian fish farms were located in sheltered coves and sounds, but such installations are now being placed out towards the open sea (above).

Fish farmers have naturally faced difficulties since modern aquaculture began in Norway just over 25 years ago. Disease and pollution had to be fought, and the big expansion in production has sometimes created over-supply and sharp price fluctuations. But substantial advances have been made in a number of areas. Breeding and improved feeds mean that a domesticated salmon reaches a weight of three-five kilograms within a year, as against two years for

its wild cousin. Research programmes have also made it possible to delay the onset of sexual maturity in the fish, make them more resistant to disease and reduce feed consumption to 3.5 kilograms per kilogram of finished fish.

Fish farming will undoubtedly make further progress. Many years of research have succeeded in producing domesticated halibut in commercial quantities. Stolt Sea Farms, one of Norway's largest salmon producers, is planning to market 800 tonnes of halibut in 1997. However, it will take two-three years for larger quantities to become available. An annual output of 20 000 tonnes is forecast for 2010.

Constant trials are also being staged with farming other fish species, and it is only a matter of time before some of these are ready for marketing. But none will be as economically important as salmon.

Lobster prices are so high that farming this crustacean represents an obvious priority. The problem is that lobsters are cannibals and have to be kept isolated from each other. Automated systems for setting out and rearing lobster have now been developed. Possible sites for a first facility of this kind include Mongstad near Bergen or Tjeldbergodden in mid-Norway, which both offer warm water from Statoil plants there.

Fickle fish. Herring have changed their feeding grounds capriciously down the ages. Some 700 years ago, large shoals were found outside Bohuslän in western Sweden, but Haugesund north of Stavanger became the great herring port in modern times – until the fish moved further north. The vast catches in the winter herring fishery off the Møre coast in the 1950s have become legendary. Then the herring vanished from Norwegian waters, and has reappeared only recently. Big catches of this "sea silver" are again bringing prosperity to many fishing communities in the Møre area.

Long ago, herring was "poor folk's" food in Norway. But it is now a prized delicacy, even though the market for human consumption cannot fully absorb a really big catch. Haugesund may no longer be the home of herring, but it can at least claim the world's longest table filled with herring dishes (above left) running through the city's main streets.

Silver stream. Norway's 700 fish farms produced 249 000 tonnes of Atlantic salmon in 1995, out of a total world production of 460 000 tonnes.

A growing interest in food is perhaps a confirmation of rising prosperity, and TV programmes on cooking and culinary culture are among the most popular in Norway. The country's cuisine is rooted in domestic raw materials, but national and foreign culinary traditions have been blended to create a distinctive repertoire that is attracting attention abroad.

Champion chefs. A culinary revolution has swept through Norwegian restaurants over the past few decades. Several are now honoured with one or more stars in Michelin's world-famous guide. And Norway's team in the main international chef's competitions has celebrated one triumph after another.

Norwegian chefs are naturally at their best with dishes based on marine raw materials – mollusks, crustaceans and fish. This page presents some delicacies from the sea: fish soup (top), a salmon and prawn composition (above) and salmon in dill ready for the grill (left).

Kelp cutters. Virtual forests of kelp and seaweed flourish along the Norwegian coast. Pronova Biopolymer utilises only five per cent of these reserves, but ranks nevertheless among the world's leading alginate producers. The company's special trawlers cut the kelp mechanically in waters between two and 15 metres deep. This is a renewable resource, and can be harvested again after five years.

Large-scale industrial production of alginates is a relatively new process, and Pronova can supply more than 200 different varieties of this product. They are used as additives in food, pharmaceuticals, textile dyes, dental supplies and paper. Gels, dressings, ice cream, fruit compotes, jams, marmalades, fruit juices, sweets and beer are among the many food industry products that benefit from alginates.

More from fewer. As in other industrialised countries, Norway's agricultural sector has experienced sweeping changes. The number of farmers has declined sharply, from 210 000 in 1945 to 86 000 today.

Less than 30 000 of these are solely employed on the land. On the other hand, they produce more than ever and make Norway self-sufficient in most livestock products.

Freer markets and ever-growing food imports mean that Norwegian farmers are finding it ever harder to compete. Neither the climate nor the size of their farms encourage large-scale operation.

Farming in a mountain country far to the north and in competition with agricultural produce from southern climes is a big challenge. Many countries are better suited to animal husbandry or growing grain and vegetables than Norway. Small farms often lie scattered far up the fjords, with snow-clad mountains and precipitous valley slopes as their nearest neighbours. The Nærlands Fjord (above) in western Norway's Sogn district is a case in point. Elsewhere, farms located high on the valley sides towards the naked mountaintops have a very short growing season.

Broad acres. Norwegian agriculture is not confined to mountain farms or smallholdings in the north and west, where cultivation must normally be combined with fishing or other employment. The best farming regions are characterised by well-run holdings managed along the same lines as in other countries. Grain is the most important produce from these farms.

Flavourful fruit. Extraordinary flavours and aromas can be achieved in all fruit and berries grown close to the limits of their range. That certainly applies to fruit and berries in Norway. Many people predict a

fine future for these delicacies in export markets, not only because of their intense flavour but also because they mature at different times than in European countries further south.

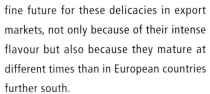

Free flocks. Sheep play an important role for farmers in some parts of Norway, and are crucial for settlement in many rural communities. Few domesticated animals live such untrammelled lives as Norwegian sheep, with some 2.5 million of them wandering freely all summer in forest, field and mountain. The bells worn by the grazing animals can be heard tinkling day and night, from the time the flocks are released in May until they are fetched home in the autumn. These sheep have no idea what feed concentrates are. Spending several months in the open, with plenty of natural fodder and a lot of exercise, ensures that their wool and meat achieve particularly high quality. Norwegian chefs, at least, swear by domestic lamb. Many motorists on Norway's roads meet the scene on the left during the autumn months, as sheep are brought down from the pastures.

Water of life. Aquavit is the national spirit of the Scandinavian countries, and its production rests on ancient traditions. Denmark, Norway and Sweden compete to offer the best brands. All are based on potato spirit, but Norwegians remain convinced that their aquavits achieve greater flavour and a more rounded quality than those from the neighbouring nations. The most famous of all aquavits is Linie, so called because it travels to and from Australia across the Equator (or "line") in old sherry casks on ships operated by Wilh Wilhelmsen before being bottled and sold. Not enough of this brand can be produced to meet demand. A selection of Norwegian aquavits is displayed above.

Wide woods (preceding pages). Productive forests cover more than a fifth of Norway, and the raw materials they provide have been a key factor in the country's industrialisation. From the Middle Ages, timber exports yielded substantial revenues. It has even been claimed that King Harald Hårfagre (Fairhair) was able to unite Norway into a single realm 1 100 years ago because export earnings from timber allowed him to raise an army.

Fit to print. Farming and forestry are closely related in Norway, and forest land makes a substantial contribution to farm incomes. The Norwegian pulp and paper industry has been through a major restructuring over the past 30 years under the leadership of Norske Skog. As the country's largest group in this sector, the latter was founded at the initiative of Norwegian forest owners. It began to produce newsprint on a modest scale at Nordenfjeldske Treforedling in Skogn on the Trondheim Fjord in 1966. This mill (left) now has an annual capacity of 540 000 tonnes. Thirteen of Europe's 20 largest daily papers get their newsprint from Nordenfjeldske.

Norske Skog has gradually developed into the dominant company in Norway's pulp and paper sector. It also has mills in France and Austria, and produces 2.4 million tonnes of printing papers annually to rank as the world's fifth largest manufacturer of such products.

Modern veteran. Saugbrugsforeningen in Halden, which now belongs to Norske Skog, is a veteran in Norway's paper industry. A completely new mill for magazine paper has the same annual capacity – 540 000 tonnes – as the group's newsprint mill in Skogn. The picture above is from the new magazine paper machine at the mill in Halden south of Oslo.

Cardboard containers. It is many years since glass milk bottles were phased out in favour of cardboard cartons in Norway. These beverage containers are environment-friendly because 80 per cent of the materials in them can be recycled. A new recycling facility will make cardboard con-

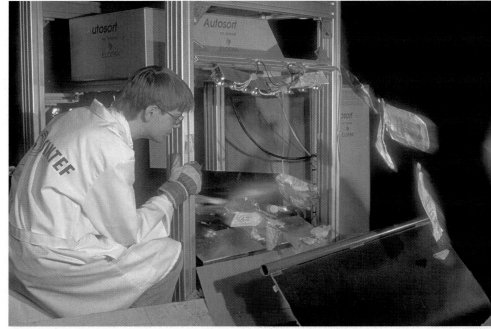

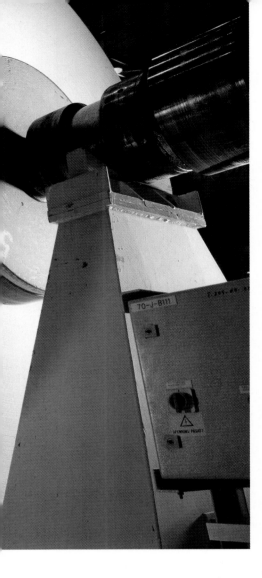

tainers even more attractive, manufacturer Elopak believes. Owned by Norway's dominant tobacco company, Tiedemann, this company originally produced its cartons under a US licence but ended up buying out the licensor and developing a leading position in the cardboard packaging field. Elopak has plants in many European countries and recorded NOK 3.2 billion in 1995 revenues.

Packaging accounts for roughly half the waste in an average household. Together with the Sintef research foundation, Elopak has developed a machine (left) that uses infra-red sensors to sort beverage containers from a continuous flow of waste.

A new Tiedemann company, Autosort, has been established to produce and market this unit. It is already operating in Germany, which imposes very strict rules for sorting and recovering packaging. Similar regulations are likely to be adopted in other countries, so the market for sorting equipment could expand strongly.

The recycling process turns used cartons into office products with a relatively high value.

OUT IN THE OPEN

Norway is a relatively big country with a small population. At a time when people in polluted cities are keener than ever to gain free access to nature and outdoor life, Norwegians take open-air leisure activities for granted both summer and winter.

Nature shapes character. Norway's general barrenness made it a land of diligent and conscientious people – at least until the oil came. They say Norwegians seldom rest until they have fulfilled an incredible range of commitments. If nothing urgent remains to be done, they think up a few forms of self-torment – long trips through forest and mountains on skies or by foot, and all kinds of endurance test. They head for the woods with power saws and axes to fell trees, or spend days and nights hunting or fishing.

The need felt by so many Norwegians to earn life's pleasures, and their inability to relax in the sun or by the fireside until they have scaled at least the nearest peaks, are viewed as part of the national character.

Tourists who want to do things quickly and easily, and who are seeking sun, warmth and beaches, should go elsewhere. Norway is a place for people wanting to encounter the challenge and drama of nature in mountain, in forest or at sea. Few countries witness such seasonal variation in natural conditions, with rain clouds never far away along the western coast. Landscapes vary from peaceful farming districts and deep forests in the east to fjords and thousands of islands facing the open sea to the west.

Moving from a sunny island realm along the southern coast to Norway's northernmost county, Finnmark, truly represents a long leap. The unspoiled wilderness of Finnmark, Europe's last exotic travel destination, is best known for its reindeer and opportunities for hunting and fishing. But most people are unaware that this region can experience the hottest summer temperatures in Europe for weeks on end.

Norway has few rivals when it comes to combining tourism with nature. In 1996, Germany's Holiday magazine hailed Norway as the world's best country in this respect. A jury of 250 executives from German travel agencies, tour operators, travel organisations and travel journalists agreed that Norway has achieved a successful balance between commercial tourism and protection of the environment.

Not for tourists. The Lofoten islands are a favourite tourist destination, but few visitors fortunately attempt to emulate this climber on Svolværgeita. Performed high above Svolvær, largest town in the islands, such a leap certainly looks far from safe.

Great to be young. Norway is a good place to be a child. Most people live outside the city centres, giving their children a natural playground right outside the front door. Youngsters normally spend their days outside whatever the season, but are always dressed to cope with the weather.

Rainwear keeps children dry even when the playground is a waste of muddy puddles. Lifejackets are standard attire by the sea or in boats. And quilted trousers and jackets combat the cold when building snowmen or snow castles, or when skiing. Such garments have become Norwegian specialities, with a natural place in a child's wardrobe.

Ski skills. Skiing occupies a large place in Norwegian hearts. Of course, not everyone in Norway dons their skis the minute the first snowflakes settle, and very few would be willing to follow the skier jumping off a mountain in Hemsedal (right). But woods and fields can get crowded when young and old set off on their weekend ski outing, with babies drawn in sleds. And the whole nation is kept virtually glued to the TV set during the big international winter sports contests. Competitors who return with Olympic gold medals or as world champions can become national heroes.

Subsea garden. Many kinds of plant flourish on the seabed along the Norwegian coast. The underwater garden on the preceding pages is from the Idde Fjord, which forms the southern border with Sweden. This inlet was long so polluted that all submarine life died out, but an extensive environmental programme has restored both flora and fauna. Diving to view submarine scenes unlike those found in other parts of the world is one of the new activities attracting tourists to Norway.

Pleasure in boats. Tens of thousands of people take to the sea in boats of all sizes and types among the Norwegian islands during the summer. Some families spend their entire holidays cruising in comfortable motorboats or yachts, while others use small craft for daytime outings or rowing boats for fishing near their holiday cabins. Norway has a boat for every fourth man, woman and child.

With their sea sport traditions, Norwegians have been able to celebrate many victories in international regattas. Both King Harald and his late father, King Olav, represented Norway in several Olympic sailing contests. A Flying Dutchman crew trains for new international competitions (right). Incidentally, Norway's only woman to win a gold medal in the summer Olympics is a sailor – Linda Andersen, who scored her victory at the Barcelona games in 1992.

Fast and elegant. Norwegian whaling has aroused many protests from abroad, but catching whales in the Antarctic or off Norway's coasts ceased to have much significance for the national economy many years ago. More recently, many curious visitors have been attracted to whale safaris off northern Norway.

The following pages show killer whales snapped from one of the safari boats. A male killer whale can reach a length of nine metres, while females are usually half this size. With their black-and-white colouring, they are perhaps the most elegant of all the world's creatures. The killer whale eats anything and attacks even the largest animals, but is friendly towards humans. A fast swimmer, it can reach a speed of 75 kilometres per hour.

A time and a place. They say you should never invite groups to visit you from Norway at the peak of the autumn hunting season, when ptarmigan and elk are more attractive than urban commerce. Many people regard the ptarmigan hunt (preceding pages) as the highlight of their year. No less than 174 000 Norwegians took out a hunting licence in 1995, and about 100 000 of these were after ptarmigan. But this is hardly a profitable affair. Each hunter shoots only five birds on average.

Courting couple. Anyone who witnesses the capercaillie doing its courtship dance at first light on an April morning will never forget the sight. The picture on the left was taken in Nord-Østerdal in eastern Norway.

Feathered frown. Not everyone gets as close as this to a nesting Lapland owl (above).

FACING A NEW CENTURY

Aircraft, radio and TV did not exist at the beginning of this century. Anyone who had seriously suggested travelling to the moon by rocket or flying faster than sound, not to mention following wars in other continents via a screen in one's own lounge, would have been regarded either as a fantasy writer or a madman. But Jules Verne and H G Wells have long been overtaken by reality.

When aircraft made their appearance, it was proposed to close down the world's patent offices because nothing remained to invent. Serious newspapers wrote just a few years before the First World War that conflict belonged to the past because planes could bomb cities from the air. No country would dare to expose itself to such attacks.

A century later, invention has still not been exhausted. We cannot even be sure that the future will not outdo past performance. More than a thousand new ideas are submitted every year to the Norwegian Government Consultative Office for Inventors. This agency gave grants to 171 inventions in 1995 and has awarded 250 scholarships to particularly talented inventors since 1991. But only one in 10 of the concepts presented are patentable and can expect to find a market. Even fewer get through the long and demanding process that leads to the production stage.

Many inventions are the product of systematic research. So it is natural that Statoil and Norsk Hydro have been awarded more patents than any other Norwegian companies over the past two years. Some products cause sweeping change, and it is difficult to remember how we managed without computers and modern telecommunications. New technological solutions greet us on every hand. The oil industry is managing to recover oil and gas from ever greater depths, and medical research has made constant advances. Far more efficient use is being made of energy resources. Steel, aluminium, paper, glass and many other products are recycled, and wastes that previously polluted rivers and coasts form the basis for new products. These include ferro-silicon, a by-product from the important ferro-alloys industry used as a strength additive in concrete. A great deal of timber was once wasted in the pulp and paper industry, but almost all of this raw material is now utilised – not least to produce important chemical products.

Budding businesses. Kongsberg Våpenfabrikk ranked as a key high-tech company in its day, and brought together many of Norway's finest engineers. A number of smaller companies budded off from this business when it went into liquidation in 1987. They have flourished by exploiting parts of their predecessor's technology, developing and producing many exciting products. These include aircraft engine components made by Norsk Jetmotor (left).

Busy bee. Cars are among the biggest polluters of the world's cities, but electric vehicles could reduce some of these problems. They cause neither pollution nor noise. Norway has no traditions as a car manufacturer, but Oslo-based Pivco joined forces with several major Norwegian companies and institutions to design and develop the City Bee electric car. Adopted as part of the European Union's Eureka research programme, this project enjoys active support from the Norwegian authorities.

The City Bee is designed for environment-friendly urban motoring. Weighing only 700 kilograms, including batteries, it can reach a top speed of 80-90 kilometres per hour and has a range of 70-100 kilometres before the batteries need recharging. The main structural elements are made in extruded aluminium, the chassis is moulded in coloured thermoplastic and the batteries can be recycled.

Twelve prototypes of this vehicle were presented at the 1994 winter Olympics in Lillehammer, and the car is now being tested in Norway and abroad – including the city of San Francisco. Series production is due to begin in 1997.

Part production. Kongsberg Automotive is one of many Norwegian companies making parts and systems for the international car industry. A hydraulic servo clutch for the Porsche 911 Turbo is being checked on the right.

Robot revolution. Ole Molaug of Jæren Automasjonsselskap near Stavanger read an article in 1964 about the world's first industrial robots and passed the piece to Trallfa owner Nils Underhaug, among others. Underhaug wondered whether such a device could do the unhealthy and boring task of painting the wheelbarrows he produced, and Molaug's company took on the job of developing a robot.

"Ole" was installed in Trallfa's painting department on 9 February 1967, initiating a revolution that has turned the former wheelbarrow manufacturer into a world leader for painting robots. In the mid-1980s, the company became part of the international ABB Group.

A long process of development separates "Ole" from today's TR 5000, which has been installed by the world's leading car-

makers. Earlier models painted components, including car bumpers, but the present generation handles the complete chassis. About 1 500 painting robots are purchased worldwide every year, with roughly 1 000 of these supplied from Norway. The company is now ready to begin series production of handling robots. Norwegian robots paint bumpers at

one of Ford Motor's US factories in Michigan (below).

Pivoting poles. New inventions can be complex or simple. Sometimes it seems surprising that nobody has come up with an obviously good idea before, while other innovations become possible only because of technological progress.

The compliant pole for road signs (right) developed by Egill Helland shows that new patents do not necessarily derive from the computer industry and years of research. The patent covers a mechanism that allows the pole to pivot when hit by a vehicle, and spring back when the pressure has been removed. This solution could help to reduce traffic injuries and vehicle damage, and to cut today's heavy cost of replacing broken signs and foundations.

Helland has spent seven years developing the patent, which heralds a new generation of collision-friendly roadside products. The foundation unit is being marketed under the name FundaFlex.

Load-carrier. A self-powered transport system that does not run on rails is supplied by TTS of Bergen to move the largest of objects. The company claims there are no limits to the size of ship sections that can be assembled with an accuracy as high as half a millimetre. Its biggest move to date took place in Cherbourg, France, during 1993 (above left), when TTS transported the French SNLE-class nuclear submarine Le Triomphant. The transport of this 12 500-tonne vessel was witnessed directly by 13 000 people and transmitted live on French TV.

Wear well. Helly Hansen hopped onto the designer bandwagon a few years ago, and ranks today as Europe's leading producer of leisure garments. The company was best known for its rainwear, but new water-repellent materials have turned such clothes into all-weather garments. Its name has also always been closely linked with pleasure boating, and hardly a child in Norway has not worn a lifejacket with the HH label. The new survival suits found on all Norwegian fishing boats, merchant vessels and offshore ships have saved many lives, and Helly Hansen is a leading supplier of such gear. New types of suit are constantly being tested (below left).

On watch. It is a long time since unwanted visitors could sneak into Norwegian waters under cover of fog or darkness. New systems allow ship traffic to be continuously monitored (above). Kongsberg Forsvar delivers systems for command, information and weapons control on naval vessels.

Never alone. Advances in telecommunications are being made faster than anyone could have imagined, and an integration of telephony, data communications, video and other media is under way. At the beginning of 1996, 90 per cent of Norwegian industry had installed technology that allowed them to move into the age of electronic information.

Norwegian firms have won major international assignments in this sector. The state-owned Telenor telecommunications group has secured a contract to develop a paging system for 550 million people in 14 Chinese provinces, for instance. Teleplan, part of the major Norconsult consulting organisation, was given responsibility in 1978 for a large-scale development of the telephone system in Saudi Arabia. It is now handling the world's largest communications project in this country, covering 1.5 million telephone lines and a mobile phone network for 500 000 subscribers. This job has a framework of NOK 1.5 billion, making it the largest consultancy project ever accepted by a Norwegian company.

Combined GSM satellite terminals will be the future solution for anyone wanting to be available regardless of where they roam. Within a few years, such terminals are unlikely to weigh more than a kilogram. Norway's Nera presented a foretaste of such developments in 1996, with a new portable terminal weighing just 2.5 kilograms. This is almost seven kilograms lighter than earlier models. But people can already maintain contact with the rest of the world from the remotest areas of the planet, whether in the Himalayas, on the polar ice caps or in deserts (above left).

Bottle watcher. More and more countries require that glass bottles be recycled. Tomra Systems has led the development of systems for collecting returnable bottles for many years, and is one of the most exciting new companies in Norwegian industry. It began producing automated collection points for returnable bottles, and has now collaborated with the Sintef research foundation to develop a new type of self-programming unit (above). With the aid of specially-constructed optics, this machine can determine the contours of a bottle with an accuracy of 0.1 millimetres. This allows it to distinguish between bottles that look identical to the naked eye – a highly important capability given the large number of very similar bottles in circulation. The new technology is said to be very cheap to implement.

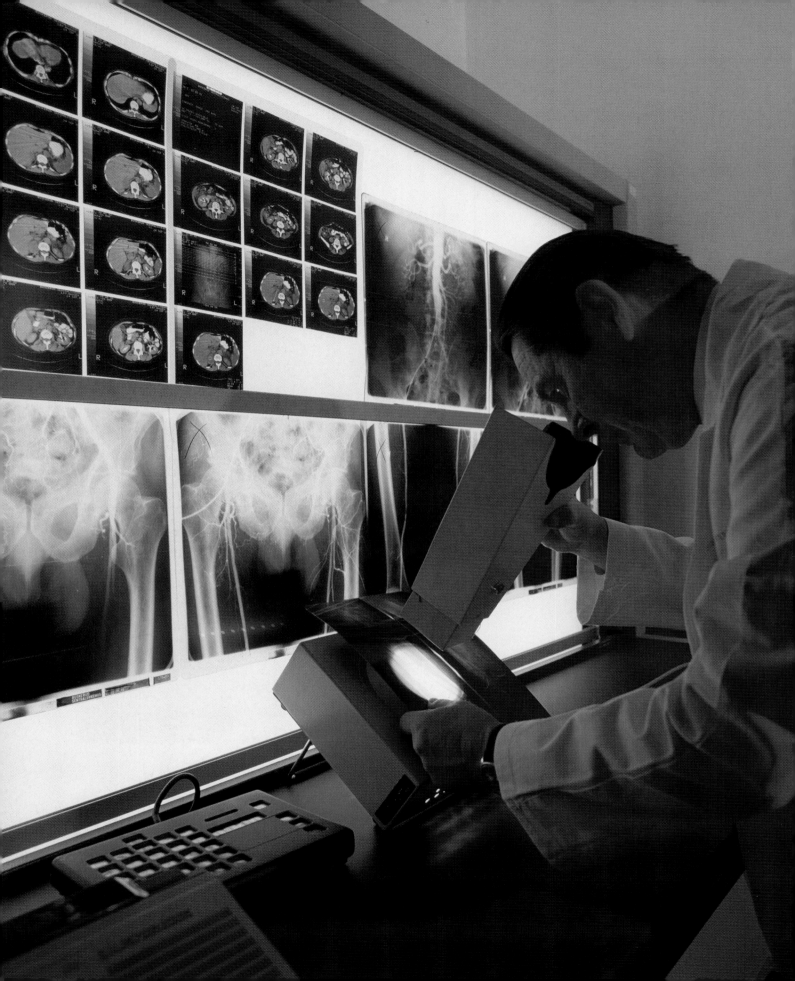

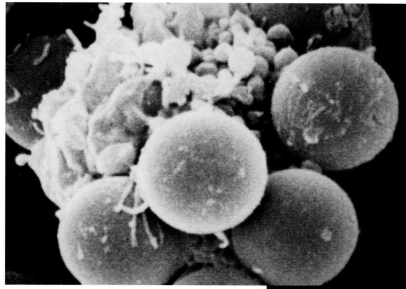

Size isn't everything. Norwegian medical science occupies the front rank in certain areas, and has made a substantial contribution. A technique for making monodisperse polymer spheres was developed by Rolf Ugelstad more than 20 years ago. These tiny but uniform particles could previously be produced only in outer space, but are now in industrial production on Earth.

Dyno Particles, a subsidiary of global explosives giant Dyno Industrier, holds the world rights to produce the Ugelstad spheres. The company has concluded collaboration deals with leading firms in a number of countries.

Clever contrasts. Nycomed has been a pioneer in developing contrast media for diagnostic imaging since the late 1970s. These preparations make it easier to use X-rays, ultrasonics and so forth to study the body's internal organs. The company pursues extensive research to maintain its global leadership in this field, which includes 42 per cent of the market for X-ray contrast media. It also aims to be a leader in therapeutic products for cancer and cardiovascular disease.

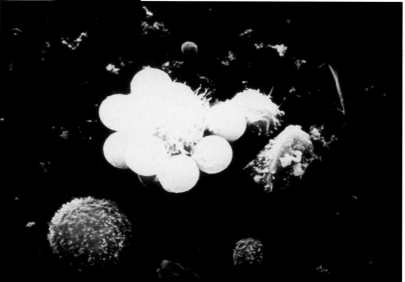

Together with Alpharma, Norway's biggest producer of antibiotics, Dyno formed the Dynal company in 1986 to exploit the biomagnetic properties of monodisperse polymer particles in the health sector. Under the Dynabeads label, they are used to separate living cells. The spheres look almost like water in their natural state, but can be used for such tasks as removing cancerous cells from bone marrow.

Dynal's goal is to develop and make products for diagnosis and treatment of cancer and other illnesses. It is collaborating with pharmaceutical companies in a number of countries, and Dynabeads have also been adapted for diagnosis and analysis of infections diseases and in the food industry.

In the heart. Vingmed Sound in Horten south of Oslo was one of three winners in a competition to find Europe's best new information technology products in 1995. Several hundred companies took part in the contest, which aimed to stimulate European IT development.

Vingmed Sound's winning entry was System Five, the product of four years of cooperation with Norwegian researchers. Backed by the Research Council of Norway, this NOK 150 million project represents the next generation of the company's family of ultrasonic imaging systems for diagnosing the cardio-vascular system.

A specialist (right) installs probe heads, one of the products in the ultrasound scanner. The smallest

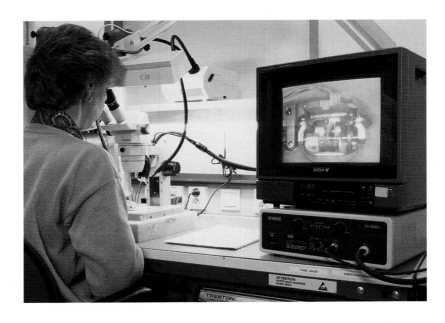

probe heads measure only nine millimetres in diameter, allowing them to be guided close to the heart through the oesophagus. This equipment has been developed in cooperation with Swiss watchmakers.

Sonic surgery. Developments in ultrasonics could revolutionise certain surgical techniques. Surgeons at the regional hospital in Trondheim, for instance, can remove brain tumours without exposing the brain. Two holes a few millimetres in diameter are made in the skull, and an ultrasonic probe is placed in one to generate images of the tumour and surrounding brain tissue that the surgeon can observe on a monitor. All changes that occur during the operation, which is conducted through the second hole, can be picked up. This approach minimises the risk of injury during brain operations, and results from a collaboration between Sintef Unimed, the regional hospital and Vingmed Sound.

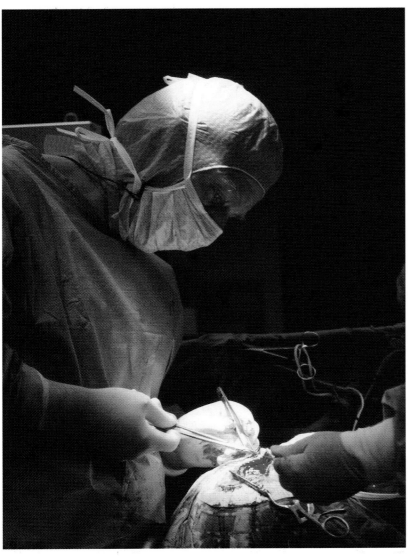

Helping save lives. This is the motto for Laerdal Medical in Stavanger, which has made a unique contribution to preventive health work. The company began life in 1940 as a toy-maker, and claimed in the early 1960s to be Europe's largest car manufacturer in terms of units produced. It then moved into the production of manikins for training people in resuscitation techniques.

When Asmund Lærdal began work on his training manikin in 1958, he wanted to make it look as much like a human being as possible. The corpse of a beautiful young girl was recovered from the Seine in Paris at the turn of the century. She remained unidentified, but a death mask was made of her. Using this mask, Lærdal created his Resusci Anne manikin. Thirty-six years after her birth, Resusci Anne is one of the world's best-known Norwegian women. Several million people have practiced resuscitation with her.

Lærdal specialises today in producing equipment to save lives, including defibrillators. When one of Australia's richest men, Kerry Packer, collapsed with a heart attack at a polo match a few years ago, an ambulance crew with a Lærdal defibrillator was on the spot within a few minutes. When Packer learned that only a few ambulances in New South Wales were equipped with such devices, he funded the purchase of 500 on condition that the authorities supplied similar equipment for the rest of the ambulances in the state. These units save 500-1 000 lives in New South Wales every year.

A WIDE WORLD BECKONS

Shipping was the only Norwegian industry with a global scope until well into the present century. With a limited home market, developing export sales was also crucial for the most important of Norway's industrial companies. But they seldom established production subsidiaries abroad because their principal products were raw materials based on domestic resources from sea, forests, rivers and waterfalls.

Major manufacturing firms in the western industrialised countries became increasingly international, and began production in all their important markets. The creation of Europe's single market and an increased level of processing by Norwegian industry meant that companies from Norway also began to move abroad in the 1960s on a far greater scale than before.

Norwegian companies cannot be called multinational in the true sense of the word, and are still small compared with the biggest industrial combines. But several of them, such as Norsk Hydro and Kværner, have achieved solid international positions by setting up or acquiring subsidiaries in the most important markets for their specialities. Since 1970, Hydro has become a substantial oil company and a global manufacturer of fertiliser and light metals. Acquiring yards around Europe has put Kværner among the world's largest shipbuilding groups in the space of a few years. Taking over Britain's Trafalgar House in 1996 also made it the largest engineering group outside the USA, with extensive operations around the world.

Many Norwegian companies have found their way onto a wider stage, including firms that started out small but succeeded in securing an international position in their niche markets. Most had no special qualifications for international success. But executives with vision and drive have won an international market position for companies such as Aker, Elkem, Helikopter Service, Luxo, Alpharma, Nycomed, Dyno and Jotun in recent decades.

The 30 largest Norwegian industrial companies in 1992 secured 64 per cent of their revenues from subsidiaries abroad. And sales from these foreign companies are rising faster than exports from Norway. At the same time, virtually the entire expansion in employment by the largest companies is taking place abroad. Only 61 per cent of jobs in the companies covered by the survey are in Norway, and this proportion is declining steadily.

Helping hand. Norway and Denmark are the only countries to have achieved the target set for the provision of development assistance by industrial nations to the Third World. Norwegian aid programmes cost about NOK 8.5 billion in 1996, more than one per cent of gross domestic product. Half this amount goes on national programmes in African countries. A large slice of Norway's spending is channelled through international organisations, but support is also given to work by Norwegian charities and local bodies in recipient countries.

Naturally, Norway provides considerable help for developing the maritime sector and hydropower, since the country has special expertise in these areas. Africa possesses some of the world's biggest hydro-electricity resources, and energy projects in this part of the world have high priority. With support from aid funds, Norwegian manufacturers have played an active role in many major African hydropower developments. These include building the continent's third largest power station, Cahora Bassa, on the Zambezi river in Mozambique (above).

Forest funding. Privately-financed Norwegian aid projects include planting new trees. The picture on the right is from a forest regeneration project in Uganda.

Outward bound. Jotun is not only Norway's dominant paint manufacturer, but also ranks as one of the world's leading suppliers of marine coatings. This company was a small domestic producer when its first foreign plant saw the light of day in Libya in 1962. Today, Jotun is one of Norway's most international groups, with 30 factories outside the country. Its expansion has been particularly strong of late in Asia and the Middle East, with four new plants starting operation in the latter region during 1995-96. Jotun's second foreign factory opened 30 years ago in Thailand, and the company has since gained a leading position in that country's paint market. Two new plants are planned to safeguard this standing.

Foreign companies accounted for 70 per cent of Jotun's 1995 revenues of NOK 5.4 billion.

The pictures on this page are from a market in Oman (right) and Dubai (above). Rein-

forced polyester from Jotun's local factory is used in the United Arab Emirates to produce new dhows, with shiny hulls emerging from the moulds to be outfitted for service in the Arabian Gulf.

Explosive expansion. Dyno Industrier was one of the first Norwegian companies to become established in south-east Asia, but has been followed by many others. Since opening in Singapore in 1970, Dyno has become one of Norway's most international groups with 100 wholly or partly owned companies in 30 countries. Three-quarters of its workforce is outside Norway, and foreign operations account for 90 per cent of revenues. The group has three business areas – explosives, chemicals and plastics, with the first of these responsible for almost half the turnover. Dyno ranks as one of the world's two largest explosives manufacturers. Prestige projects handled by the group in recent years include blasting for Hong Kong's new airport. The picture on the right is from Australia, another important market for Dyno explosives.

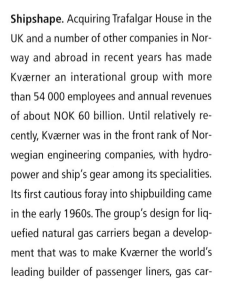

Shipshape. Acquiring Trafalgar House in the UK and a number of other companies in Norway and abroad in recent years has made Kværner an interational group with more than 54 000 employees and annual revenues of about NOK 60 billion. Until relatively recently, Kværner was in the front rank of Norwegian engineering companies, with hydropower and ship's gear among its specialities. Its first cautious foray into shipbuilding came in the early 1960s. The group's design for liquefied natural gas carriers began a development that was to make Kværner the world's leading builder of passenger liners, gas car-

riers, chemical tankers and high-speed catamarans. Thirty years on, the Kværner design for LNG ships still dominates. The group has shipyards in Norway, Finland, Germany, the UK and Singapore.

Kvaerner Govan in Scotland (above right) is one of the yards that has put the group among the world's largest shipbuilders. An LNG vessel based on Kværner's design under construction at South Korea's Hyundai Heavy Industries is pictured on the right.

Class act. Not surprisingly, Norwegian companies in the maritime sector have the best-

developed international networks. The largest is classification society Det Norske Veritas, with 280 offices in 100 countries. Almost 4 000 employees from 58 different nations work for the organisation, which provides classification, certification and consultancy services in two principal areas – shipping and offshore on the one hand and land-based industry on the other. More than 4 000 ships totalling almost 15 per cent of world tonnage are classed by DNV. Inspectors from the society check ships in Hong Kong and Brazil (top left and above left).

World-wide. The final picture in this book (following pages) gives an impression of the global scope of DNV's operations. But it can also serve to symbolise the growing internationalisation of Norwegian industry. Industrial companies in Norway are small, with a limited domestic market, and must become more international to meet competition from the major industry groups. That means more of their production must be moved abroad, a process which began late in Norway but is now well under way. And one thing is certain – this trend will continue into the next millennium.

PHOTOGRAPHS

INDEX

© Index Forlaget A/S, 1996

Design/dust jacket:
Tangen Grafiske Senter AS, Heidi Downham

Typesetting:
Tangen Grafiske Senter AS, 1996

ISBN: 82-7217-078-7